LÍNGUA INGLESA

MARIA CRISTINA G. PACHECO
Pesquisadora, licenciada em Pedagogia e Artes Plásticas; docente de língua inglesa e de língua espanhola em diversas instituições de ensino em São Paulo; autora de livros didáticos e paradidáticos em línguas estrangeiras.

MARÍA R. DE PAULA GONZÁLEZ
Docente de língua inglesa e de língua espanhola; coordenadora em vários cursos de idiomas em São Paulo.

5ª edição
São Paulo
2023

Coleção Eu Gosto Mais
Língua Inglesa 4º ano
© IBEP, 2023

Diretor superintendente	Jorge Yunes
Diretora editorial	Célia de Assis
Editores	Isabela Moschkovich e Ricardo Soares
Secretaria editorial e processos	Elza Mizue Hata Fujihara
Assistente de produção gráfica	Marcelo Ribeiro
Ilustrações	Gisele B. Libutti, Lye Kobayashi, Vanessa Alexandre
Projeto gráfico e capa	Aline Benitez
Diagramação	Nany Produções Gráficas

Dados Internacionais de Catalogação na Publicação (CIP) de acordo com ISBD

P116e   Pacheco, Maria Cristina G.

Eu gosto m@is: Língua Inglesa / Maria Cristina G. Pacheco, Maria R. de Paula González. - 5. ed. - São Paulo : IBEP - Instituto Brasileiro de Edições Pedagógicas, 2023.
il ; 20,5 cm x 27,5 cm. - (Eu gosto m@is 4º ano)

Inclui anexo.
ISBN: 978-65-5696-437-9 (Aluno)
ISBN: 978-65-5696-438-6 (Professor)

1. Educação. 2. Ensino fundamental. 3. Livro didático. 4. Língua inglesa.
I. González, Maria R. de Paula. II. Título. III. Série.

2023-1175   CDD 372.07
                                             CDU 372.4

Elaborado por Odilio Hilario Moreira Junior - CRB-8/9949

Índice para catálogo sistemático:
1. Educação - Ensino fundamental: Livro didático 372.07
2. Educação - Ensino fundamental: Livro didático 372.4

5ª edição – São Paulo – 2023
Todos os direitos reservados

Rua Gomes de Carvalho, 1306, 11º andar, Vila Olímpia
São Paulo – SP – 04547-005 – Brasil – Tel.: (11) 2799-7799
www.editoraibep.com.br   editoras@ibep-nacional.com.br
Impresso na Leograf Gráfica e Editora - Fevereiro/2025

APRESENTAÇÃO

Querido aluno, querida aluna,

Elaboramos para vocês a **Coleção Eu gosto m@is**, rica em conteúdos e atividades interessantes, para acompanhá-los em seu aprendizado.

Desejamos muito que cada lição e cada atividade possam fazer vocês ampliarem seus conhecimentos e suas habilidades nessa fase de desenvolvimento da vida escolar.

Por meio do conhecimento, podemos contribuir para a construção de uma sociedade mais justa e fraterna: esse é o nosso objetivo ao elaborar esta coleção.

Um grande abraço,

As autoras

SUMÁRIO

LESSON

1 Where are they from? 6
   (De onde eles são?)
   - **Communicative contents:** countries, nationalities and languages
   - **Grammar content:** verb *to be*

2 The history of Brazil 14
   (A história do Brasil)
   - **Communicative contents:** talking about the past; the discovery of Brazil
   - **Grammar content:** simple past

3 What did you do yesterday? 26
   (O que você fez ontem?)
   - **Communicative contents:** talking about sports
   - **Grammar content:** simple past

4 What kind of sports do you like? 36
   (De que tipo de esportes você gosta?)
   - **Communicative contents:** talking about radical sports, adventure and movies
   - **Grammar content:** verbs *to swim, to climb, to run, to dive; what kind of...?*

5 How often do you... 48
   (Com que frequência você...)
   - **Communicative contents:** talking about routines
   - **Grammar content:** adverbs of time and frequency

LESSON

6 When I was younger I used to... 58
(Quando eu era menor eu costumava…)
- **Communicative contents:** talking about frequent actions in the past
- **Grammar content:** the expression *used to*

7 Would you like to... 68
(Você gostaria de…)
- **Communicative contents:** making invitations, accepting and refusing
- **Grammar content:** conditional *tense*

8 Where are you going on your vacation? 80
(Aonde você vai nas férias?)
- **Communicative contents:** talking about actions in the near future
- **Grammar content:** adverbs and expressions of time

GLOSSARY 94
(Glossário)

COMPLEMENTARY ACTIVITIES 97
(Atividades complementares)

LESSON 1

WHERE ARE THEY FROM?
(De onde eles são?)

Listen and read.
(Escute e leia.)

Mercedes is from Bolivia.
(Mercedes é da Bolívia.)

Brian is from England.
(Brian é da Inglaterra.)

Zola is from Nigeria.
(Zola é da Nigéria.)

Noriko is from Japan.
(Noriko é do Japão.)

Pietro is from Italy.
(Pietro é da Itália.)

Rosario is from Mexico.
(Rosario é do México.)

Marc is from France.
(Marc é da França.)

Joaquina is from Portugal.
(Joaquina é de Portugal.)

João is from Brazil.
(João é do Brasil.)

ACTIVITIES

1 Research and answer the questions.
(Pesquise e responda às perguntas.)

Example:
– Where is Neymar from?
– He is from Brazil.

a) Where is Penélope Cruz from?
(Spain)

_____

b) Where are emperors Naruhito and Masako from?
(Japan)

_____

c) Where is Sade Adu from?
(Nigeria)

_____

LET'S SEE SOME NATIONALITIES AND LANGUAGES.

(Vamos ver algumas nacionalidades e línguas.)

countries (países)		nationalities (nacionalidades)	languages (línguas)
Brazil (Brasil)		Brazilian (brasileiro/brasileira)	Portuguese (português)
Argentina (Argentina)		Argentinian (argentino/argentina)	Spanish (espanhol)
Australia (Austrália)		Australian (australiano/australiana)	English (inglês)
China (China)		Chinese (chinês/chinesa)	Chinese (chinês)
England (Inglaterra)		English (inglês/inglesa)	English (inglês)
France (França)		French (francês/francesa)	French (francês)
Italy (Itália)		Italian (italiano/italiana)	Italian (italiano)
Japan (Japão)		Japanese (japonês/japonesa)	Japanese (japonês)
Mexico (México)		Mexican (mexicano/mexicana)	Spanish (espanhol)
Nigeria (Nigéria)		Nigerian (nigeriano/nigeriana)	Yoruba (iorubá)
Portugal (Portugal)		Portuguese (português/portuguesa)	Portuguese (português)
Russia (Rússia)		Russian (russo/russa)	Russian (russo)
Spain (Espanha)		Spanish (espanhol/espanhola)	Spanish (espanhol)
United States of America (USA) (Estados Unidos da América)		American (americano/americana)	English (inglês)

2 Let's play the Memory Game using different flags. Go to pages 99 and 101.
(Vamos jogar o Jogo da Memória usando diferentes bandeiras. Vá para as páginas 99 e 101.)

3 Follow the example and complete the sentences.
(Siga o exemplo e complete as frases.)

Example:
I am from France.
I am French.

a) I am from _____.

　　I am _____.

b) He is from _____.

　　He is _____.

c) I am from _____.

　　I am _____.

d) She is from _____.

　　She is _____.

e) And you? Where are you from? Draw your country's flag.
(E você? De onde você é? Desenhe a bandeira do seu país.)

I am from _____. I am _____.

4 Search and select one of the celebrities on page 103. Cut and glue, then check what country this person was born in and some movies that he or she starred.
(Pesquise e escolha uma das celebridades na página 103. Recorte e cole a foto no espaço reservado e, em seguida, assinale em qual país esta pessoa nasceu e alguns filmes que estrelou.)

☐ Mexico   ☐ France

☐ England ☐ Israel

☐ USA   ☐ Australia

10

5 Read the text and answer true (**T**) or false (**F**).
(Leia o texto e responda verdadeiro ou falso.)

Maria	– Hello, Joe!
Joe	– Hi, Maria! This is my friend Gabriela.
Maria	– Hi, Gabriela! Nice to meet you. Where are you from?
Gabriela	– I am from Argentina. And you, Maria?
Maria	– I am Brazilian. You are from Canada, aren't you?
Joe	– No. I'm American. I'm from the USA.

          T   F

a) Joe and Maria are friends.

b) Maria and Gabriela are friends.

c) Gabriela is Argentinian.

d) Maria is Brazilian.

e) Joe is from Mexico.

11

6 Listen and answer true (**T**) or false (**F**) to the statements.
(Escute e responda verdadeiro ou falso.)

	T	F
a) Peter, Mark and Greg are friends.	☐	☐
b) Peter is from Spain.	☐	☐
c) Peter and Mark are from Australia.	☐	☐
d) Greg is from Australia.	☐	☐
e) Mark and Greg speak French.	☐	☐

Now, connect each of the boys with their country flag.
(Agora, ligue cada menino à bandeira de seu país.)

| Mark | Peter | Greg |

7 Complete the chart with the languages spoken in each country.
(Complete o quadro com as línguas faladas em cada país.)

China (China)	_____	England (Inglaterra)	_____
Japan (Japão)	_____	France (França)	_____
Portugal (Portugal)	_____	Italy (Itália)	_____
Nigeria (Nigéria)	_____	Russia (Rússia)	_____
Argentina (Argentina)	_____	Spain (Espanha)	_____

8 Let's practice. Follow the example.
(Vamos praticar. Siga o exemplo.)

> **Example:**
> Lewis Hamilton is from England.
> He speaks English.

a) Messi is from Argentina.

He speaks _____.

b) I'm from Brazil.

I speak _____.

c) Taylor Lautner is from the USA.

He speaks _____.

13

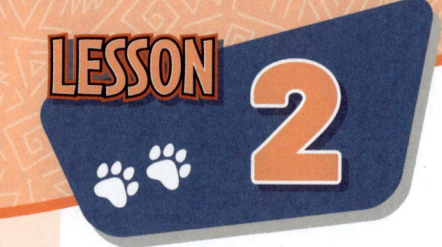

THE HISTORY OF BRAZIL
(A história do Brasil)

Listen and read.
(Escute e leia.)

Cabral arrived in Brazil in 1500. Watercolor (1900) of Alfredo Roque Gameiro, a Portuguese painter.

The arrival of Cabral in Brazil

Cabral named this land Terra de Vera Cruz. The winds were strong and the ships found a safe place here. They called it Porto Seguro.

The Portuguese met the **natives**, who lived in the territory and were the **owners** and **rulers** of the land. Some of them resisted and attacked the **foreigners**, others **agreed** and cooperated with them.

Cabral ordered to build a **cross** and **claimed** the area for Portugal. A **mass** was celebrated by the **priests**.

Pero Vaz de Caminha wrote a letter about this discovery to King Manuel, and Cabral sent a ship with this letter back to Lisbon.

VOCABULARY

afraid of: com medo.
agreed: concordaram.
claim: reivindicar (verbo).
cross: atravessar (verbo).

foreigners: estrangeiros.
mass: missa.
natives: nativos.
owners: donos

peaceful: pacífico.
priests: sacerdotes.
rulers: líderes, quem manda.
strangers: estranhos.

Attention!
(Atenção!)

Usamos o **simple past** para falar de algo que aconteceu no passado.

Examples:

- I **studied** History yesterday.
  (Eu estudei história ontem.)
- He **went** to a restaurant last night.
  (Ele foi a um restaurante ontem à noite.)
- Cabral **arrived** in Brazil in 1500.
  (Cabral chegou ao Brasil em 1500.)
- Juscelino Kubitschek **founded** Brasilia in 1960.
  (Juscelino Kubitschek fundou Brasília em 1960.)

ACTIVITIES

1 Read the text and say if it is true (**T**) or false (**F**).
(Leia o texto e diga se é verdadeiro ou falso.)

		T	F
a)	Cabral first named this land Brazil.	☐	☐
b)	The Portuguese met the natives.	☐	☐
c)	The natives were the owners of the land.	☐	☐
d)	The natives were afraid of the strangers.	☐	☐
e)	Pero Vaz de Caminha wrote a letter about the discovery to King Manuel.	☐	☐

15

2 Go to page 14. Underline the verbs in the text and fill out the chart in the simple past.
(Vá para a página 14. Sublinhe os verbos no texto e preencha a tabela no tempo passado.)

to agree		to live	
to attack		to meet	
to be		to name	
to call		to order	
to claim		to resist	
to cooperate		to send	
to find		to write	

READ THIS VERB LIST.
(Leia esta lista de verbos.)

VERBS		
verb	simple past	translation
to arrive	arrived	chegar
to come	came	vir
to declare	declared	declarar
to discover	discovered	descobrir
to found	founded	fundar
to go	went	ir
to learn	learned	aprender
to play	played	jogar, brincar, tocar
to read	read	ler
to sign	signed	assinar
to stay	stayed	ficar
to study	studied	estudar
to travel	traveled	viajar
to visit	visited	visitar
to watch	watched	assistir
to work	worked	trabalhar

3 Underline the verbs. Change the simple past to the present tense. Translate both sentences.
(Sublinhe os verbos. Mude o passado simples para o tempo presente. Traduza as duas frases.)

> **Example:**
>
> I **played** video games yesterday.
> Eu joguei *video game* ontem.
>
> I **play** video games every day.
> Eu jogo *video game* todo dia.

a) I traveled to the beach last week.

b) Susan studied Math at school.

c) My father lived in England in the 80's.

d) My grandparents came to Brazil in 1956.

17

4 These important events happened in Brazil. Complete with the verbs in the simple past.
(Estes eventos importantes aconteceram no Brasil. Complete com os verbos no passado.)

a) Cabral _____ in Brazil in 1500. (arrive)

b) D. Pedro I _____ the Independence of Brazil in 1822. (declare)

c) The slavery abolition in Brazil was _____ by Princess Isabel in 1888. (sign)

d) Brasilia was _____ in 1960. (found)

5 Match the sentences.
(Ligue as sentenças.)

a) Where did you travel to? ☐ I played video games yesterday.

b) Where did Cabral arrive? ☐ I traveled to the beach last week.

c) What did Susan study? ☐ Susan studied Math last night.

d) When did you travel to Rio? ☐ Columbus discovered America.

e) What did you play? ☐ Cabral arrived in Brazil.

f) What did Columbus discover? ☐ I traveled to Rio last month.

Attention!
(Atenção!)

last: último.
last month: mês passado.
last night: ontem à noite.
last week: semana passada.
last year: ano passado.
yesterday: ontem.

6 Let's write the sentences correctly.
(Vamos escrever as frases corretamente.)

a) last month at school / Brazilian History / I studied

_____

b) to Lisbon / last year / I traveled

_____

c) my grandparents / I visited / last night

_____

d) for the last test / I studied / a lot

_____

e) video games / I played / yesterday

___

f) you learn / last week? / at school / What did

___

g) you do / What did / last summer?

___

h) last year / in Uruguay / She lived

___

7 Check (✓) the correct alternative.
(Marque ✓ a alternativa correta.)

a) ☐ I stay at home yesterday.

☐ I stayed at home yesterday.

b) ☐ Mary and I studied for the test last night.

☐ Mary and I study for the test last night.

c) ☐ She traveled to Bahia last summer.

☐ She travel to Bahia last summer.

d) ☐ You go to the beach last year.

☐ You went to the beach last year.

e) ☐ They watched TV yesterday.

☐ They watch TV yesterday.

21

Brazil: a country made by immigrants

Where did your grandparents come from? Do you know people from other countries?

Nobody lived in the American continent 30.000 years ago: Early natives came from Asia, Afro-Brazilians came from Africa, and immigrants came from Europe.

All Americans, and Brazilians too, are a mixture of peoples from everywhere.

8 Read the text and underline all the simple past tense verbs.
(Leia o texto e sublinhe todos os verbos no passado.)

Italian immigrants in coffee farm. The late nineteenth century.

My favorite person

My **great-grandfather** was born in Italy. He came to Brazil when he was six years old with his parents and brothers. He worked in a big coffee farm and he went to a small school. He learned about the culture, the food and the language of Brazil.

9 Are any of your great-grandparents alive?
(Algum dos seus bisavós está vivo?)

☐ Yes   ☐ No

Talk to your parents, and write the name of your maternal and paternal great-grandparents.
(Converse com seus pais e escreva o nome dos seus bisavós maternos e paternos.)

Attention!
(Atenção!)

great-grandfather: bisavô.
great-grandmother: bisavó.
great-grandparents: bisavós.

_____ _____
_____ _____
_____ _____

10 Write about the person you like most.
(Escreva sobre a pessoa de quem você mais gosta.)

_____
_____
_____
_____
_____
_____
_____
_____
_____

REVIEW
(Revisão)

I can ask people where they are from.
(Eu sei perguntar de onde as pessoas são.)

– Where are you from?
– I **am from** Belo Horizonte.

1 Answer the questions. What's your nationality?
(Responda às questões. Qual a sua nacionalidade?)

a) Where are you from? **(Canada)**

_____

b) Where are you from? **(Japan)**

_____

c) Where are you from? **(Spain)**

_____

d) Where are you from? **(United States of America)**

_____

2 Connect the countries to the languages.
(Relacione os países aos seus idiomas.)

a) Brazil, Portugal   ☐ Russian

b) England, United States of America   ☐ French

c) France   ☐ Portuguese

d) Italy   ☐ Italian

e) Spain, Argentina, Mexico   ☐ Japanese

f) Japan   ☐ Spanish

g) Russia   ☐ English

I learned some verbs in the present and in the past.
(Eu aprendi alguns verbos no presente e no passado.)

Present	Past	Translation
attack	attacked	atacar
discover	discovered	descobrir
eat	ate	comer
find	found	encontrar, descobrir
found	founded	fundar
go	went	ir
play	played	jogar, brincar, tocar
study	studied	estudar
travel	traveled	viajar
write	wrote	escrever

3 Put the sentences in order and change the verbs to simple past.
(Ordene as frases e passe os verbos para o passado.)

a) Alexander Flemming / in / **discover** / penicillin / 1928

_____

b) pirates / The / **find** / the / treasure

_____

c) soccer / **play** / Pelé

_____

d) the / **eat** / They / sandwiches

_____

25

LESSON 3
WHAT DID YOU DO YESTERDAY?
(O que você fez ontem?)

Listen and read.
(Escute e leia.)

We went to the club.
(Nós fomos ao clube.)

Brian swam in the pool.
(Brian nadou na piscina.)

The boys played soccer.
(Os garotos jogaram futebol.)

Fred read a book.
(Fred leu um livro.)

We went to a restaurant.
(Nós fomos a um restaurante.)

They had a barbecue.
(Eles fizeram um churrasco.)

ACTIVITIES

1 Let's listen and write what these people did in the past.
(Vamos escutar e escrever o que estas pessoas fizeram no passado.)

a) Mark _____ soccer.

b) John _____ at the beach.

c) Anna _____ a book.

d) Gabriel _____ tennis yesterday.

Attention!
(Atenção!)

Os verbos no passado têm formas diferentes. Os verbos regulares terminam sempre em **-ed** e os irregulares têm terminações variadas.
Exemplos:

Regulares

- **Play**
  I **played** soccer.
  He **played** soccer.

- **Study**
  I **studied** English.
  He **studied** English.

Irregulares

- **Eat**
  I **ate** a sandwich.
  She **ate** a sandwich.

- **Read**
  I **read** a book.
  She **read** a book.

- **Swim**
  I **swam** in the pool.
  He **swam** in the pool.

- **Begin**
  I **began** to understand.
  She **began** to understand.

27

LET'S SEE SOME SPORTS.
(Vamos ver alguns esportes.)

soccer
(futebol)

Anderson played
soccer yesterday.
(Anderson jogou futebol ontem.)

tennis
(tênis)

Jane won an important tennis
competition last month.
(Jane venceu uma importante competição de tênis no mês passado.)

volleyball
(volei)

Silvia played volleyball
last week.
(Silvia jogou vôlei na semana passada.)

swimming
(natação)

Phill swam in the pool
this morning.
(Phill nadou na piscina hoje de manhã.)

handball
(handebol)

Our team lost the handball
competition last year.
(Nosso time perdeu a competição de handebol no ano passado.)

basketball
(basquete)

John played basketball
last Sunday.
(John jogou basquete domingo passado.)

2. Let's find the sports.
(Vamos encontrar os esportes.)

soccer   tennis   basketball   volleyball   swimming   handball

T	U	I	V	B	E	K	L	O	P	B	A	N	M
V	S	A	M	X	G	W	J	V	Y	G	M	A	B
A	A	T	S	N	N	I	N	O	Z	S	K	B	S
L	C	V	B	L	L	K	E	L	Z	L	L	A	W
L	C	N	A	X	S	T	H	L	A	L	N	E	I
O	R	C	S	D	O	K	T	E	N	N	I	S	M
C	E	N	T	U	C	E	S	Y	R	Y	N	I	M
K	R	O	D	X	C	G	H	B	G	B	S	S	I
E	B	A	S	K	E	T	B	A	L	L	B	A	N
N	F	P	Q	F	R	Z	J	L	A	L	A	L	G
C	O	H	A	N	D	B	A	L	L	F	B	L	R
N	I	N	O	Z	S	K	T	E	N	D	B	A	L

3. Let's discuss and answer.
(Vamos discutir e responder.)

a) What sports do you like?

_____

b) And your best friend? What sports does he/she like?

_____

c) And your teacher? What sports does he/she like?

_____

d) And your father? What sports does he/she like?

_____

4 Connect the verbs to the actions.
(Ligue os verbos às ações.)

to relax

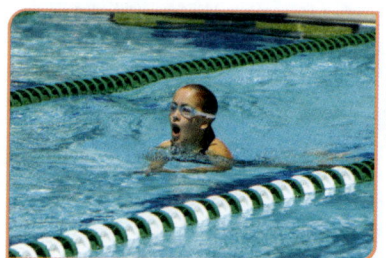

MICHAEL BRAUN

to drink

POLKA DOT IMAGES

to play soccer

STOCKBYTE

to swim

WOJCIECH GAJDA

to eat

DONATELLA TANDELLI/ SHUTTERSTOCK

to play tennis

GETTY IMAGES

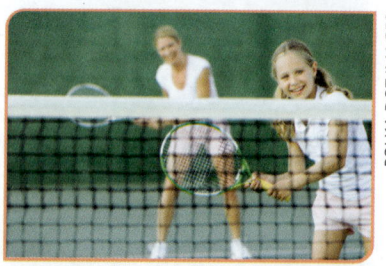

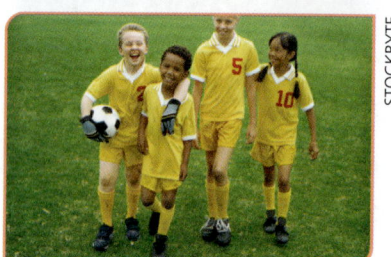

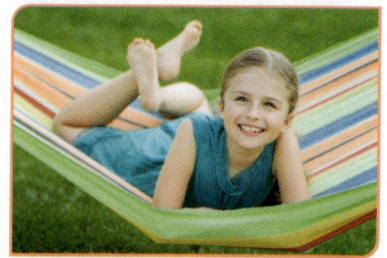

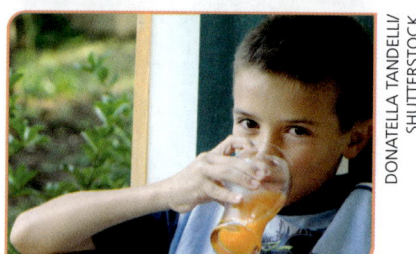

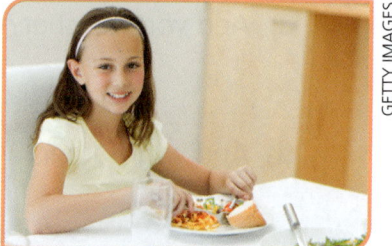

5 Choose the appropriate verbs from the box to fill in the blanks.
(Escolha os verbos apropriados para preencher os espaços em branco.)

| went | relaxed | played | read |

a) Yesterday I _____ to the club.

b) Wilson _____ a very funny book last weekend.

c) My sister _____ tennis and at night she _____ in the garden.

6 Rewrite the sentences from exercise 5 in the present tense.
(Reescreva as frases do exercício 5 no presente.)

a) _____

b) _____

c) _____
_____

7 Choose one of these actions and draw it.
(Escolha uma das ações e faça um desenho dela.)

8 Listen and check (✓) what you hear.

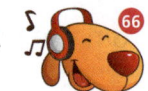

(Escute e marque o que você ouve.)

BRIAN MCENTIRE

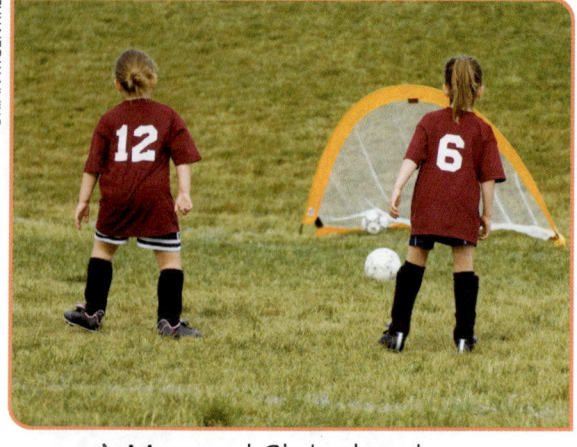

a) Mary and Chris played

- [ ] tennis.
- [ ] volleyball.
- [ ] soccer.

JUPITERIMAGES

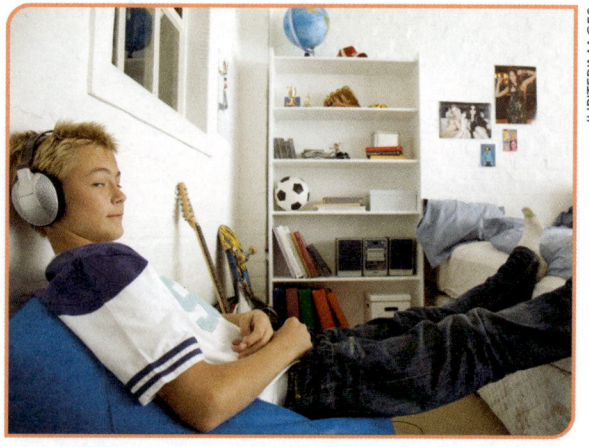

b) Peter

- [ ] relaxed.
- [ ] sat in the chair.
- [ ] organized the bedroom.

GETTY IMAGES

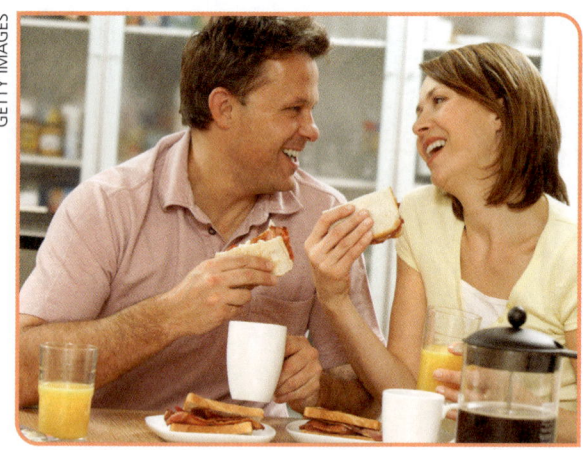

c) My mom and dad

- [ ] read a book.
- [ ] talked.
- [ ] ate sandwiches.

ADRIAN BROCKWELL

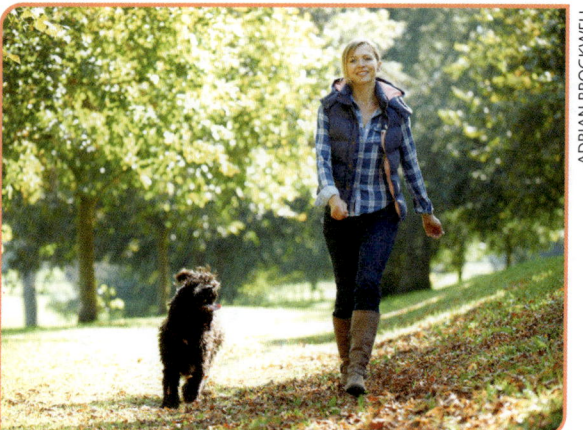

d) My aunt Meggy

- [ ] studied Math.
- [ ] walked in the park.
- [ ] swam.

9 Match the verbs to their translations.
(Ligue os verbos às suas traduções.)

a) see ☐ escutar, ouvir

b) eat ☐ assistir

c) read ☐ ver

d) swim ☐ escrever

e) play ☐ imaginar

f) watch ☐ comer

g) imagine ☐ acreditar

h) believe ☐ nadar

i) listen ☐ ler

j) write ☐ jogar, brincar

10 Now, write the verbs in the past.
(Agora, escreva os verbos no passado.)

> relaxed   swam   played   ate
> saw   read   wrote   watched

a) see (ver) _____

b) eat (comer) _____

c) swim (nadar) _____

d) watch (assistir) _____

e) relax (relaxar) _____

f) play (jogar/brincar) _____

g) read (ler) _____

h) write (escrever) _____

11 Cut, glue and complete.
(Recorte, cole e complete.)

Example:

jogar

play / played

MASTER1305/SHUTTERSTOCK

comer ______________________

estudar ______________________

nadar ______________________

ver ______________________

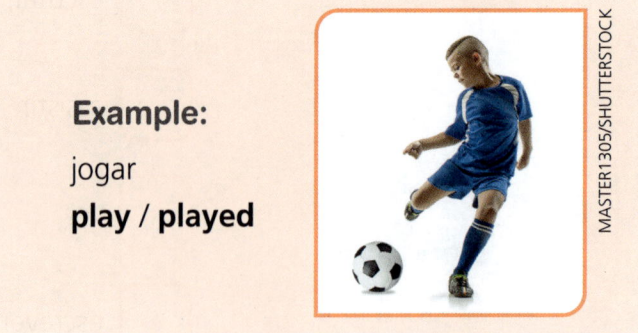

12 Separate the verbs in the present and in the past.
(Separe os verbos no presente e no passado.)

Verbs	Present		Past	
to believe	I		I	
to eat	you		you	
to go	he		he	
to imagine	she		she	
to listen	I		I	
to play	you		you	
to read	she		she	
to relax	I		I	
to see	you		you	
to sit	she		she	
to study	you		you	
to swim	she		she	
to walk	I		I	
to watch	he		he	
to write	she		she	

35

WHAT KIND OF SPORTS DO YOU LIKE?
(De que tipo de esportes você gosta?)

EXTREME SPORTS
(Esportes radicais)

Listen and read.
(Escute e leia.)

rafting

windsurf

diving

climbing

rappel

skiing

ACTIVITIES

1 Read the text and answer the questions.
(Leia o texto e responda às perguntas.)

A lot of people like sports. Some people like sports with excitement, emotion and high risks. They don't want to play soccer, swim or ride a bike. They are looking for something else. They want ADVENTURE!

Climbing, windsurfing, rafting, rappelling, motocross are considered extreme sports and to practice a radical sport you have to be well-prepared, strong and healthy. And don't forget to get a good coach.

Text written especially for this book.

Motocross is a extreme sport.

a) What are the extreme sports mentioned in the text?

_____, _____, _____,

_____ and _____.

b) What do you need to practice a extreme sport?

I have to be well- _____, _____, _____

and get a _____.

c) According to the text, do you need a person to help you with this practice?

_____.

2 Check (**T**) or false (**F**).
(Marque verdadeiro ou falso.)

a) Everybody likes extreme sports. ☐

b) A lot of people like sports. ☐

c) Some people want adventure. ☐

3 Match!
(Relacione!)

a) rafting ☐

b) diving ☐

c) cycling ☐

d) soccer ☐

e) running ☐

f) rappel ☐

38

4 Read the text and answer the questions.
(Leia o texto e responda às perguntas.)

Brazil loves sports: Surf!

There are famous professional Brazilian surfers nowadays, like Gabriel Medina, for example, but surfing is more popular as an amateur sport. Brazil has several beaches suitable for it, and it is one of the most popular extreme sports in the country. It is hard not to find a surfer while you are visiting a Brazilian beach. Variations of this sport – like Bodyboarding and Standup Paddle – are also popular.

Gabriel Medina surfing in Bali, Indonesia.

a) The name of a famous surfer.

_____.

b) Names of surf variations.

_____.

VOCABULARY

Also: também
Amateur: amador
Like: como
Nowadays: atualmente
Several: muitos, diversos
Suitable: apropriadas

Attention!
(Atenção!)

- I liked
- you liked
- he liked

- I didn't like
- you didn't like
- he didn't like

- she liked
- we liked
- they liked

- she didn't like
- we didn't like
- they didn't like

39

5 Unscramble the sentences.
(Ordene as frases.)

a) _____
   (I / diving / didn't / like)

b) _____
   (rafting / like / didn't / She)

c) _____
   (They / windsurf / didn't / like)

d) _____
   (didn't / climbing / You / like)

e) _____
   (didn't / motocross / We / like)

6 Let's answer. Follow the example.
(Vamos responder. Siga o exemplo.)

> **Example:**
> – What kind of sports do you like?
> (De quais tipos de esporte você gosta?)
> – I like soccer and basketball.
> (Eu gosto de futebol e de basquete.)

a) What kind of sports does your sister/brother like?

   He/She likes _____.

b) What kind of sports does your mother like?

   She likes _____.

c) What kind of Olympic sports do you like?

   I like _____.

LET'S TALK ABOUT MOVIES. DO YOU LIKE IT?
(Vamos conversar sobre filmes. Você gosta?)

Example:

– What kind of movies do you like?
(De que tipo de filmes você gosta?)

– I like cartoon movies.
(Eu gosto de filmes de desenho.)

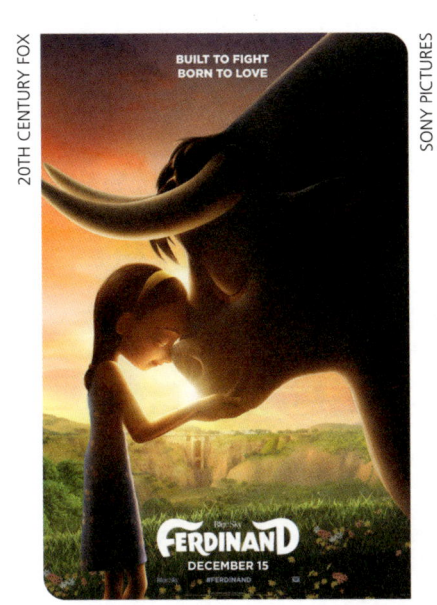

cartoon
(desenho animado)

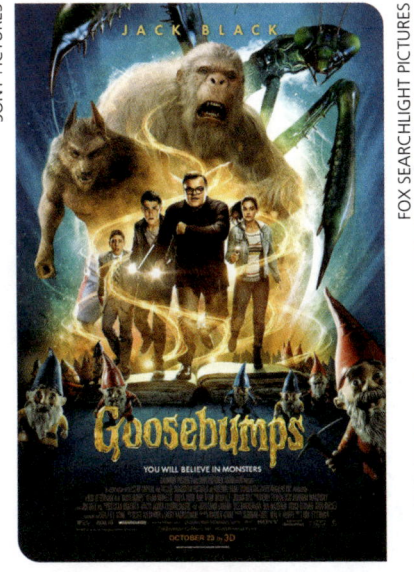

comedy
(comédia)

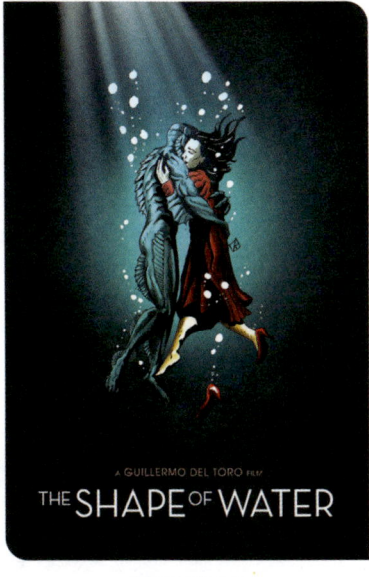

romance
(romance)

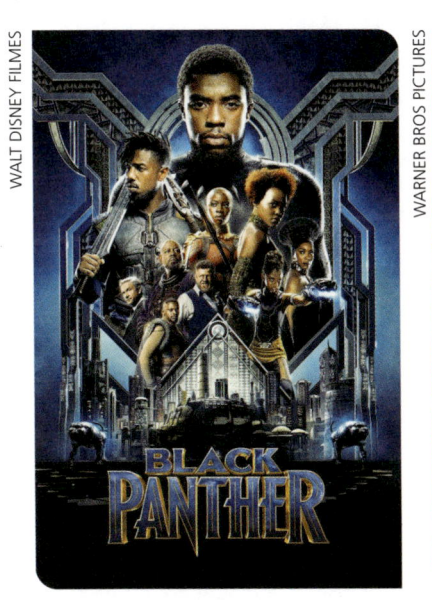

action
(ação)

science fiction
(ficção científica)

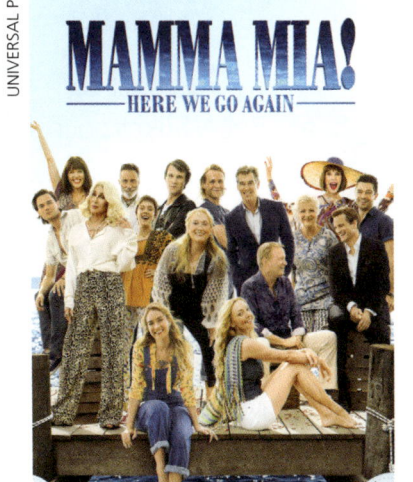

musical
(musical)

41

7 Let's investigate.
(Vamos investigar.)

a) What kind of movies do you like?

I _____.

b) What kind of movies do your parents like?

They _____.

c) What kind of movies does your best friend like?

He/She _____.

8 Listen and mark true (**T**) or false (**F**) according to the dialogue.
(Escute e marque verdadeiro ou falso de acordo com o diálogo.)

	T	F
a) Robert likes soccer.	☐	☐
b) Mark likes soccer and basketball.	☐	☐
c) Mark is 8.	☐	☐
d) Mark is American.	☐	☐
e) They like all kinds of sports.	☐	☐

9 Copy the sentences you marked false (**F**) in exercise 8. Put them into the negative form.
(Copie as sentenças que você marcou como falsas no exercício 8. Coloque-as na forma negativa.)

_____

_____

_____

10 Let's find out the sports and movies some people like.
(Vamos pesquisar esportes e filmes de que algumas pessoas gostam.)

Sports

a) My mother likes _____.

b) My father likes _____.

c) My teacher likes _____.

d) My best friend likes _____.

e) My brother likes _____.

Movies

a) My grandfather likes _____.

b) My grandmother likes _____.

c) My cousin likes _____.

d) I like _____.

e) My uncle likes _____.

43

11 Survey. Go to page 105.
(Pesquisa. Vá para a página 105.)

12 Let's write down the results of the survey.
(Vamos escrever os resultados da pesquisa.)

    a) Most of my colleagues like to drink _____

_____.

    b) Most of my colleagues like to eat _____

_____.

    c) The kind of movies most of my colleagues like is _____

_____.

    d) The kind of sports most of my colleagues like is _____

_____.

    e) The kind of dessert most of my colleagues like is _____

_____.

13 Find six words and define the topic they belong to.
(Encontre seis palavras e defina o tópico ao qual elas pertencem.)

A	C	T	I	O	N	Z	C	O	B	A	N	C	E	V	A
M	Y	A	T	P	T	B	O	Q	O	D	T	S	J	K	C
I	K	O	T	R	U	W	M	A	C	A	O	T	M	P	O
N	S	C	I	E	N	C	E	F	I	C	T	I	O	N	A
C	V	U	N	Y	E	H	D	C	A	R	T	O	O	N	C
M	U	S	I	C	A	L	Y	C	M	A	F	L	N	B	M

_____

44

REVIEW
(Revisão)

> **I learned some more verbs in the simple past tense.**
> (Eu aprendi mais alguns verbos no *simple past tense*.)
>
> - **Play**
>   I **played** soccer.
>   He **played** soccer.
> - **Eat**
>   I **ate** a sandwich.
>   She **ate** a sandwich.
> - **Swim**
>   I **swam** in the pool.
>   He **swam** in the pool.

1 Connect the verb to their sentences in the simple past tense.
(Ligue o verbo às suas sentenças no passado.)

eat	I saw a red door.
swim	She ate an apple.
watch	You read a book.
believe	They swam in the river.
write	I played soccer.
see	He watched television.
read	She imagined a story.
play	I believed you.
imagine	I listened to a music.
listen	You wrote a letter.

2 Write three other sentences using the simple past with the verbs above.
(Escreva outras 3 frases usando o passado simples com os verbos acima.)

_____

_____

_____

45

I can talk about these sports.
(Eu sei falar sobre estes esportes.)

| soccer | volleyball | running | windsurfing | climbing | rappel |
| tennis | basketball | rafting | diving | running | skiing |

3 Name a Brazilian athlete who won an international medal in one of these sports we talked about. Draw and write about him/her.
(Pesquise um atleta brasileiro que tenha ganhado uma medalha internacional em um dos esportes estudados. Ilustre e escreva sobre ele/ela.)

I can talk about these kinds of movies.
(Eu sei falar destes tipos de filmes.)

| cartoon | romance | science fiction |
| horror | action | musical |

4 What's the last movie you saw? Name it and write the kind of movie it is and its main character. Illustrate and write about the movie.
(Qual foi o último filme a que você assistiu? Diga o título, o tipo de filme e os personagens principais. Desenhe e escreva sobre o filme.)

LESSON 5

HOW OFTEN DO YOU...
(Com que frequência você...)

Listen and read.
(Escute e leia.)

...take a shower?
(toma banho?)

...brush your hair?
(escova seu cabelo?)

...wash your hands?
(lava suas mãos?)

...make your bed?
(arruma sua cama?)

...wash the dishes?
(lava a louça?)

...clean your room?
(limpa seu quarto?)

...brush your teeth?
(escova seus dentes?)

...go to school?
(vai para a escola?)

...do your homework?
(faz sua lição de casa?)

ACTIVITIES

1 Match the letters to the symbols, find the actions and illustrate them.
(Relacione as letras com os símbolos, encontre as ações e ilustre-as.)

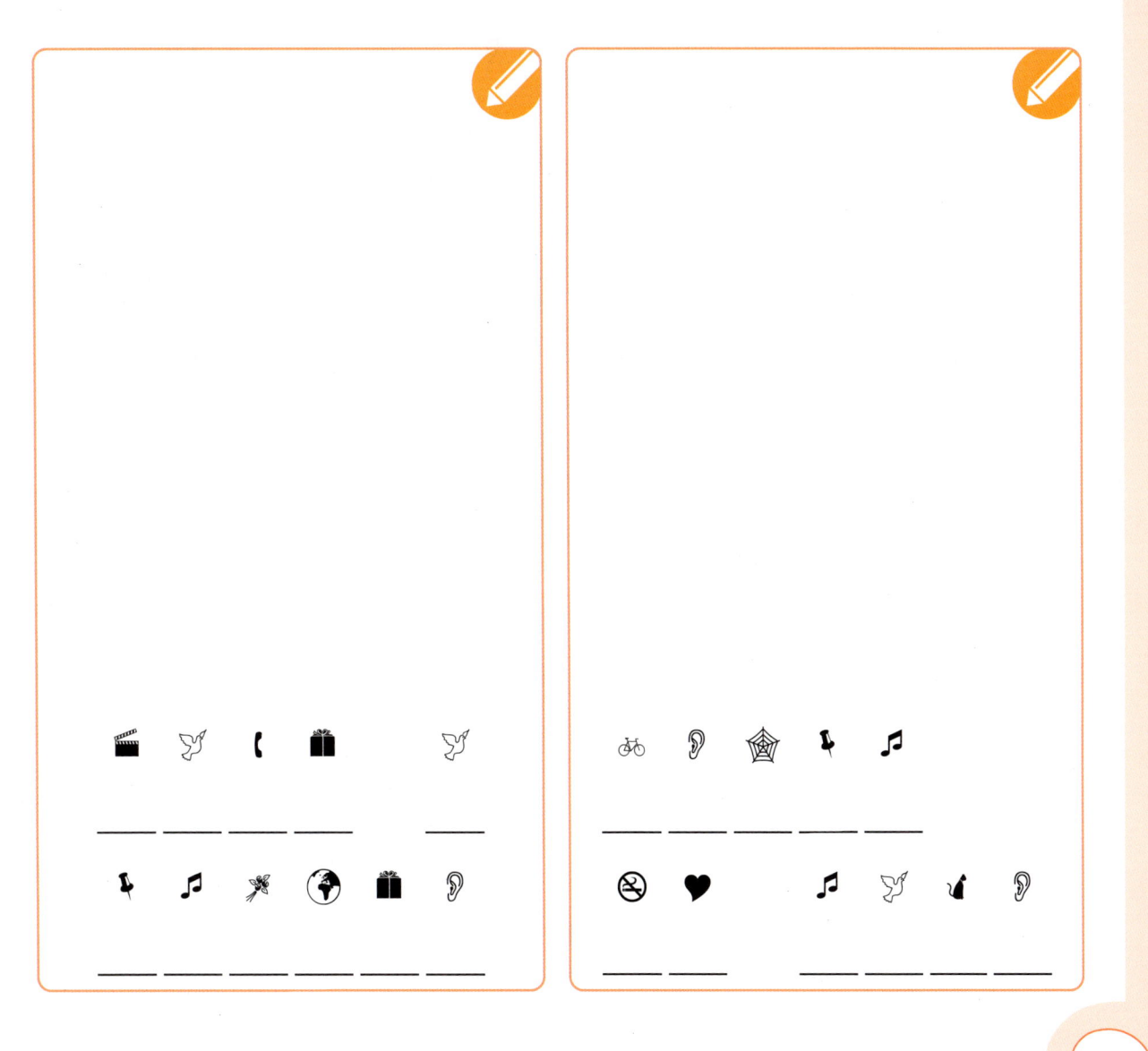

2 Match the pictures to the actions.
(Relacione as imagens às ações.)

a) go to school
b) wash the dishes
c) wash your hands
d) brush your hair
e) make the bed
f) clean your room
g) do your homework
h) brush your teeth
i) go to the club

50

Attention!
(Atenção!)

Os **frequency adverbs** são usados para indicar a frequência com que realizamos determinadas ações.

- **always:** sempre
- **sometimes:** às vezes
- **never:** nunca
- **every day:** todo dia

David goes to school **every day**.

Mary **never** drinks soda.

They **sometimes** go to a soccer game.

Brenda **always** does her homework.

Barbara **sometimes** washes the dishes.

3 Let's think and answer how often we do the following activities.
(Vamos pensar e responder com que frequência fazemos as seguintes atividades.)

	always	sometimes	never	every day
go to school (ir à escola)				
wash the dishes (lavar a louça)				
wash hands (lavar as mãos)				
brush the hair (escovar o cabelo)				
make the bed (arrumar a cama)				
clean the room (limpar o quarto)				
do the homework (fazer a lição de casa)				
brush teeth (escovar os dentes)				
go to the club (ir ao clube)				

4 Let's translate.
(Vamos traduzir.)

a) sempre _____

b) às vezes _____

c) nunca _____

d) todo dia _____

52

5 Let's talk and write. Follow the examples.
(Vamos conversar e escrever. Siga os exemplos.)

> **Examples:**
> – How often do you go to school?
> (Com que frequência você vai à escola?)
>
> – I go to school every day.
> (Eu vou à escola todos os dias.)
>
> – How often do you go to the club?
> (Com que frequência você vai ao clube?)
>
> – I sometimes go to the club.
> (Eu às vezes vou ao clube.)

a) – How often do you play board games?

– I _____.

b) – How often do you make your bed?

– I _____.

c) – How often do you watch TV?

– I _____.

d) – How often do you do your homework?

– I _____.

e) – How often do you wash the dishes?

– I _____.

f) – How often do you make the bed?

– I _____.

g) – How often do you clean your bedroom?

– I _____.

6 Interview a friend and tell the class what you found out.
(Entreviste um amigo e conte à classe o que você descobriu.)

Example:

Do your homework.
- My friend Beatrice does her homework every day.

Go to school.
- I go to school every day.
- He/she goes to school every day.

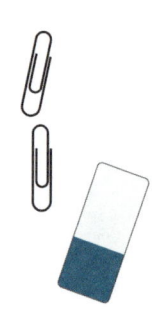

does   makes
cleans   goes
plays   dances
washes   brushes

Attention!
(Atenção!)

his/her = dele/dela

a) Make your bed.

_____
_____
_____

b) Clean your room.

_____
_____
_____

c) Go to the movies.

_____
_____
_____

d) Play soccer.

e) Dance.

f) Wash the dishes.

g) Watch TV.

h) Brush your teeth.

i) Play with friends.

7 Let's color to show how often you do the following activities.
(Vamos colorir para mostrar a frequência com que você faz as seguintes atividades.)

🟥 never 🟨 sometimes 🟦 always 🟩 every day

8 Let's cut, match and glue the pairs. Go to page 107.
(Vamos cortar, relacionar e colar os pares. Vá para a página 107.)

LESSON 6

WHEN I WAS YOUNGER I USED TO...
(Quando eu era menor eu costumava...)

Listen and read.
(Escute e leia.)

When I was seven years old, I used to go to school in the afternoon.
(Quando eu tinha sete anos, costumava ir à escola à tarde.)

When Peter was a baby, he used to drink a lot of milk.
(Quando Peter era bebê, ela costumava tomar muito leite.)

When Lily was three years old, she used to ride a tricycle.
(Quando Lily tinha três anos, ela costumava andar de triciclo.)

When I was one year old, I used to use a pacifier.
(Quando eu tinha um ano, costumava usar uma chupeta.)

58

Attention!
(Atenção!)

Para falar de coisas que aconteciam no passado, usamos a expressão: **used to**.

Examples:

- Paul **used to** go to school.
  (Paul costumava ir à escola.)

- Mary **used to** study English with a private teacher.
  (Mary costumava estudar inglês com um professor particular.)

- She **used to** eat a lot of ice cream.
  (Ela costumava tomar muito sorvete.)

When my brother was 8 years old, he **used to** sleep late.
(Quando meu irmão tinha 8 anos, costumava dormir tarde.)

When my cousin was 7 years old, she **used to** watch cartoons.
(Quando minha prima tinha 7 anos, costumava assistir a desenhos animados.)

ACTIVITIES

1 Write sentences using **used to**.
(Escreva frases usando *used to*.)

Example:

10 / study in the morning

When she **was** 10 years old, she **used to** study in the morning.

9 / used to have swimming lessons

a) When she _____ _____, she _____ _____.

7 / used to have soccer training

b) When he _____ _____, he _____ _____.

60

8 / used to play with her grandmother

c) When she _____

_____, she _____

_____.

4 / used to play with toy cars

d) When he _____

_____, he _____

_____.

2 / used to sleep with a teddy bear

e) When he _____

_____, he _____

_____.

2 Find out who used to do what and write about it.
(Descubra quem costumava fazer o que e escreva sobre isso.)

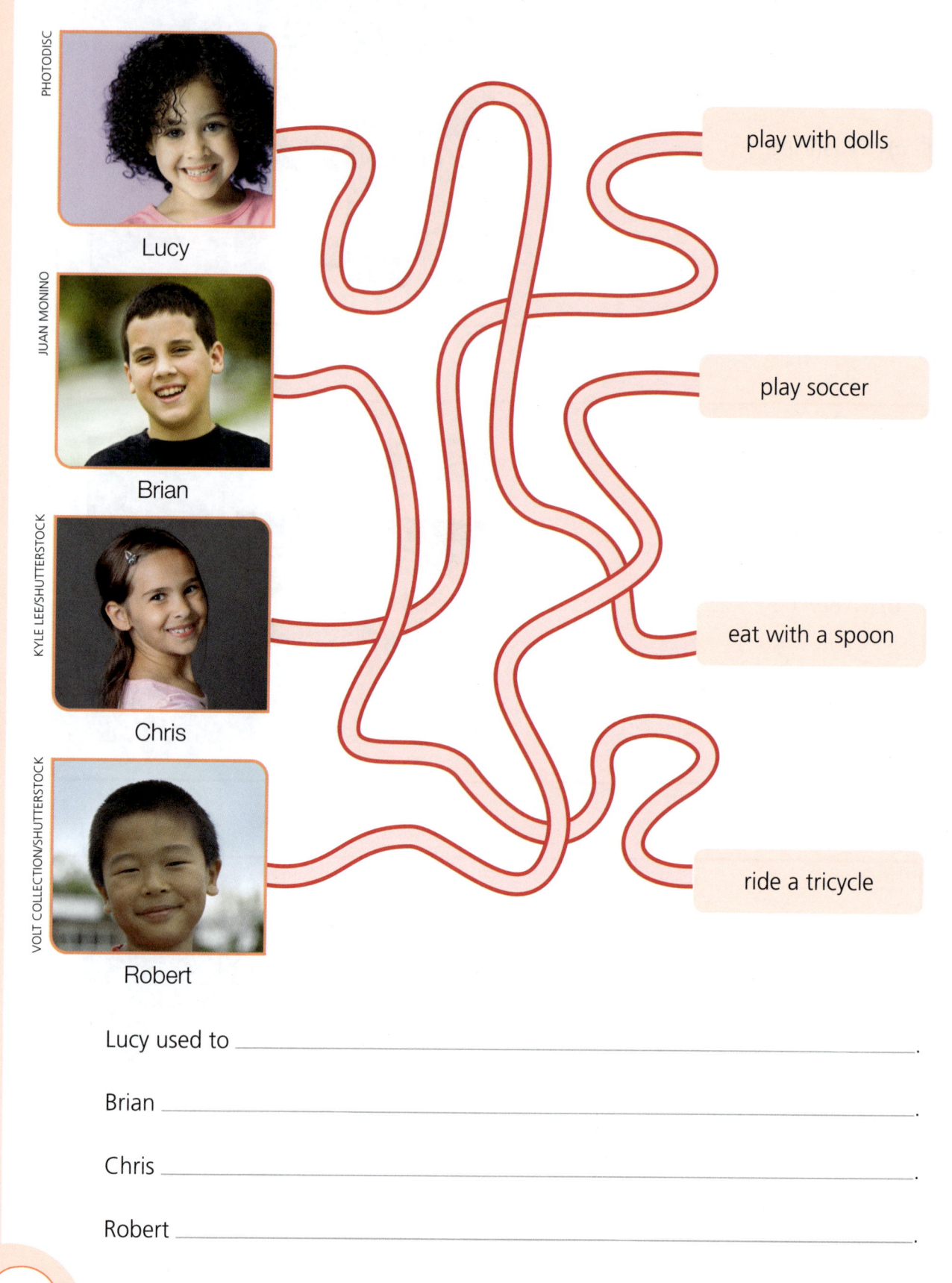

Lucy

Brian

Chris

Robert

play with dolls

play soccer

eat with a spoon

ride a tricycle

Lucy used to _____.

Brian _____.

Chris _____.

Robert _____.

62

3 Ask your mother three things she used to do when she was a little girl, and write them here.
(Pergunte à sua mãe três coisas que ela costumava fazer quando era pequena e escreva-as aqui.)

_____

_____

_____

And now ask your father.
(Agora pergunte ao seu pai.)

_____

_____

_____

4 Choose one of the actions and make a drawing of it.
(Escolha uma das ações e desenhe-a.)

My mother/father used to _____.

63

5 Let's put the sentences in the negative form. Follow the example.
(Vamos colocar as sentenças na forma negativa. Siga o exemplo.)

> **Example:**
> I **used to** ride a tricycle.
> I **didn't use to** ride a tricycle.

a) I used to use a pacifier.
_____

b) He used to play soccer with his friends.
_____

c) She used to go to the supermarket with her parents.
_____

d) They used to study Math for a test.
_____

e) My brother used to watch cartoons every day.
_____

6 Listen and match the sentences.
(Escute e ligue as frases.)

When she was a baby,	he used to go to the movies.
When I was a child,	she used to take a bottle.
When he was a teenager,	I used to watch TV in the afternoon.

VOCABULARY

take a bottle: tomar mamadeira.

64

7 Go to page 109. Select an action that you used to do and another one that you didn't. Cut and glue, then write using **used to** e **didn't use to**.
(Vá para a página 109. Escolha uma ação que você costumava fazer e outra que não costumava fazer. Recorte e cole, depois escreva utilizando *used to* e *didn't use to*.)

REVIEW
(Revisão)

> **I learned to talk about the frequency of actions.**
> (Eu aprendi a conversar sobre a frequência das ações.)
>
> Never, sometimes, every day and always.
>
> Example:
> – How often do you go to the beach?
> – I **always** go to the beach.

1 Complete the questions and write the answers.
(Complete as perguntas e escreva as respostas.)

a) – How often does Jane _____ English? **(study)**

– She _____. **(always)**

b) – How often do you _____ to school? **(go)**

– I _____. **(always)**

c) – How often does your mother _____ chocolate? **(eat)**

– My mother _____. **(usually)**

d) – How often does your brother _____ soccer? **(play)**

– He _____. **(never)**

e) – How often does your cousin _____ to the movies? **(go)**

– He _____. **(sometimes)**

f) – How often do you _____ your teeth? **(brush)**

– I _____. **(three times a day)**

I learned to talk about things I used to do.
(Eu aprendi a conversar sobre coisas que costumava fazer.)

– I **used to** play with my friends.

2 Write and illustrate things you used to do when you were a little child.
(Escreva e desenhe coisas que você costumava fazer quando era criança.)

67

LESSON 7

WOULD YOU LIKE TO...
(Você gostaria de...)

Listen and read.
(Escute e leia.)

...swim in the pool at the club?
(...nadar na piscina no clube?)

...visit a museum?
(...visitar um museu?)

...play soccer with me?
(...jogar bola comigo?)

...go to my uncle's farm?
(...ir à fazenda de meu tio?)

...go to my birthday party?
(...ir à minha festa de aniversário?)

...go to a barbecue?
(...ir a um churrasco?)

...play in my house?
(...brincar na minha casa?)

...go to the beach?
(...ir à praia?)

68

ACTIVITIES

1 Find five words.
(Encontre cinco palavras.)

F	H	K	R	N	F	Q	Q	X	P
B	E	A	C	H	A	P	P	I	O
W	U	L	C	F	R	Y	Y	M	K
T	X	A	Y	T	M	L	L	U	I
L	D	M	N	W	S	I	Q	S	S
C	C	I	O	P	J	O	D	E	A
L	A	B	A	R	B	E	C	U	E
U	U	K	L	D	K	Z	W	M	V
B	B	A	T	O	M	A	T	J	O

Check (✓) what you found.
(Marque o que você achou.)

☐ beach   ☐ barbecue   ☐ museum   ☐ party

☐ house   ☐ restaurant   ☐ club   ☐ farm

Now, write an invitation using one of the words you found.
(Agora, escreva um convite usando uma das palavras que você encontrou.)

_____

69

2 Let's make and answer invitations. Then, talk and write.
(Vamos fazer e responder convites. Depois, vamos conversar e escrever.)

Yes, thanks.
(Sim, obrigado.)

I'm sorry, I can't.
(Sinto muito, não posso.)

Examples:
– **Would you like** to go to my birthday party?
– Yes, thanks.

– **Would you like** to go to my birthday party?
– I'm sorry, I can't.

a) – Would you like to _____
_____?
– _____.

go to a restaurant

b) – Would you like to _____
_____?
– _____.

go to the beach

c) – Would you like to _____
_____?
– _____.

go to a farm

70

d) – Would you like to _____ ?

– _____ .

study in my house

e) – Would you like to _____ ?

– _____ .

play outside

f) – Would you like to _____ ?

– _____ .

go to the movies

g) – Would you like to _____ ?

– _____ .

go to the club

71

3 Write the sentences correctly.
(Escreva as frases corretamente.)

a) Would you / the mall / on Friday? / like to go to

_____

b) card games / like to play / after school? / Would you

_____

c) Would you / dance presentation? / like to go to my

_____

d) my basketball / like to watch / Would you / game?

_____

e) you like / my beach house? / to go to / Would

_____

4 Write invitations. Follow the example.
(Escreva convites. Siga o exemplo.)

Example:

Dear friend,
I would like to invite you to my birthday party.
Tomorrow, November 9th, at 7 o'clock
at my house at 384 Michigan Avenue.

Mary

STOCKIMAGEFACTORY.COM/SHUTTERSTOCK

SERHII BOBYK/SHUTTERSTOCK

5 Listen and match the dialogues.
(Escute e relacione os diálogos.)

Would you like to come to my house?

Would you like to swim this afternoon?

Would you like to play a new video game?

Would you like to go to a barbecue?

No, thanks. I am a vegetarian.

No thanks, I don't like video games.

Yes, it is very hot.

Yes, I would like to go to your house.

75

ACCEPTING AND REFUSING INVITATIONS.
(Aceitando e recusando convites.)

Look at these examples.
(Veja esses exemplos.)

> Would you like to go to a barbecue?

> Yes, thanks.

Inviting to a barbecue.
(Convidando para um churrasco.)

> Would you like to come to my house?

> No, I'm sorry. I can't.

Inviting to go to your house.
(Convidando para ir à sua casa.)

6 Write dialogues.
(Escreva diálogos.)

a)

b)

77

7 Listen and complete the dialogues.
(Escute e complete os diálogos.)

a) – Would you like to ☐ go to the movies? ☐ go to my party?

– Yes, thanks. Where is it?

– It's at 384 Michigan Avenue.

b) – Would you like to go to my house?

☐ – Yes, very much.   ☐ – No, I'm sorry, I can't.

c) – Would you like to ☐ go to the zoo? ☐ go to the club?

– Oh, sorry, I can't.

d) – Would you like to go to a party tomorrow?

☐ – Yes, thanks.   ☐ – No, I'm sorry, I can't.

8 Write new dialogues based on the ones you listened.
(Escreva novos diálogos com base nos que você escutou.)

a) _____

_____

b) _____

_____

_____

c) _____

_____

_____

9 Create more dialogues inviting people. Follow the indications for refusing or accepting the invitations.
(Crie mais diálogos convidando pessoas. Siga as indicações de recusa ou aceitação dos convites.)

a) [YES]   b) [YES]   c) [NO]

a) – _____

– _____

b) – _____

– _____

c) – _____

– _____

10 Would you like to participate in the Project Gymkhana of Solidarity?
(Você gostaria de participar do Projeto Gincana de Solidariedade?)

☐ Define the following information:
- What kind of clothes can be donated?
- Who are we helping with the donations?
- Which is the deadline for the reception?

☐ Let's organize a campaign of solidarity collecting clothes.

☐ Create different pieces of advertising and fix them in the main common areas.

☐ Find a special place, boxes or any other specific containers.

☐ Define the organization which will receive the donations.

VOCABULARY
Advertising: avisos/propaganda
Campaign: campanha
Clothes: roupas
Containers: recipientes
Donations: doações

LESSON 8

WHERE ARE YOU GOING ON YOUR VACATION?
(Aonde você vai nas férias?)

Listen and read.
(Escute e leia.)

I am **going to** a farm.
(Vou para uma fazenda.)

I am **going to** a summer camp.
(Vou para um acampamento de verão.)

I am **going to** the mountain.
(Vou para a montanha.)

I am **going to** the beach.
(Vou para a praia.)

> **Attention!**
> (Atenção!)
>
> Future continuous: é usado para falar de planos para o futuro.
> Examples:
> - I am **going to** the club.
> - You **are going to** a party.
> - He **is going to** my house.
> - She **is going to** school.
> - We **are going to** the dentist.
> - They **are going to** the apartment.

ACTIVITIES

1 Complete the answers with the **going to** form.
(Complete as respostas com a forma *going to*.)

> **Example:**
> – Where **are you going** on your vacation?
> – I **am going to** the beach.

a) – Where is he going on his vacation?

– He _____ to the farm.

b) – Where are they going on their vacation?

– They _____ to Salvador.

c) – Where is she going on her vacation?

– She _____ to the beach.

d) – Where are we going on our vacation?

– We _____ to the mountains.

Attention!
(Atenção!)

When? (Quando?)
- **next weekend:** próximo fim de semana
- **tomorrow:** amanhã
- **next week:** próxima semana
- **next month:** próximo mês

2 Translate the adverbs and create sentences describing your plans.
(Traduza os advérbios e crie frases descrevendo seus planos.)

a) próximo fim de semana: _____.

b) amanhã: _____.

c) próxima semana: _____.

d) próximo mês: _____.

3 Complete the sentences with the adverbs of time.
(Complete as sentenças com os advérbios de tempo.)

a) We are going to the club _____.

b) They are going to school _____.

c) He is going to a restaurant _____.

d) We are going to 5th grade _____.

e) My grandfather is coming to visit me _____.

4 Listen, write the alternatives and complete the sentences.
(Escute, escreva as alternativas e complete as frases.)

– Where is Peter going next Sunday?

– _____.

– Where are you going next Saturday?

– _____.

– Where are Rebeca and Paul going tomorrow?

– _____.

– Where are Marc and Jack going next weekend?

– _____.

83

5 Let's answer the questions and illustrate their answers.
(Vamos responder às questões e ilustrar as respostas.)

a) Where are you going next weekend?
(Aonde você vai no próximo fim de semana?)

_____

b) Where are you going tomorrow?
(Aonde você vai amanhã?)

_____

c) Where are you going next week?
(Aonde você vai na semana que vem?)

d) Where are you going next month?
(Aonde você vai no mês que vem?)

6 Let's write where these people are going to. Look at the example.
(Vamos escrever para onde estas pessoas vão. Observe o exemplo.)

soccer game	beach	party	barbecue	~~club~~
(jogo de futebol)	(praia)	(festa)	(churrasco)	(clube)

Example:

He is going to the club.

a) _____.

86

b) _____.

c) _____.

d) _____.

87

7 Go to page 111. Cut and glue four actions below and write sentences using **going to**.
(Vá para a página 111. Recorte e cole quatro ações abaixo escreva frases usando *going to*.)

8 Let's find the adverbs of time.
(Vamos encontrar os advérbios de tempo.)

U	T	Z	Y	M	E	K	F	W	X	P	R	T	X
X	E	P	X	B	R	Y	J	E	K	M	F	T	F
E	X	N	E	X	T	W	E	E	K	E	N	D	E
N	D	A	T	L	O	H	U	O	V	S	E	B	W
A	M	S	I	B	M	C	G	H	X	C	N	K	C
V	T	M	K	P	O	R	L	W	N	M	E	T	H
W	H	J	N	G	R	F	E	D	V	L	C	B	K
D	W	F	T	E	R	G	F	X	W	T	W	A	E
N	E	X	T	M	O	N	T	H	M	I	N	N	X
Z	N	F	H	G	W	Q	J	H	O	D	E	C	T
G	R	U	N	E	C	S	R	E	E	R	X	W	N
E	E	O	R	M	T	Z	L	E	W	W	T	B	F
Q	V	N	A	X	T	Y	O	K	T	H	W	Y	E
K	P	P	V	G	J	N	E	X	T	Y	E	A	R
Y	I	H	Q	R	P	T	S	P	A	V	E	Q	X
O	L	G	J	W	Q	B	M	K	S	D	K	Y	Y

9 Write what you found.
(Escreva o que você achou.)

_____   _____

_____   _____

89

NEXT MONTH IS VACATION TIME.
(No próximo mês é tempo de férias.)

Interview your colleagues and take notes so you can talk to them on your vacation.
(Entreviste seus colegas e anote tudo para que você possa falar com eles durante as férias.)

Name (nome)	Phone number (telefone)

Enjoy your vacation!
(Aproveite suas férias!)

10 Vacation time. Read the text and match the pictures to the items on this list.
(Período de férias. Leia o texto e relacione as imagens com os itens da lista.)

If you are staying home for your vacation, here are some ideas:

1. Play in the mud. It's messy, but it's one of the best ways to have fun of all time!

2. Make forts using pillows, blankets and couch cushions.
   It's a load of fun. Bonus challenge: Make the fort large enough for grown-ups!

3. Watch movies at home. Popcorn and lemonade are good snacks.

4. Study the weather. Set up a little weather station and measure rainfall and temperature. Write it down during your vacations and compare with your friends when you go back to school.

VOCABULARY

Blankets: lençóis
Changes: muda
Couch cushions: almofadas
Discover: descobrir, descubra
Enough: suficiente
Grown-ups: adultos

Measure: medida
Messy: bagunçado
Mud: lama
Pillows: travesseiros
Rainfall: chuva
Weather: clima

91

REVIEW
(Revisão)

I learned how to receive and make invitations. (Eu aprendi como receber e fazer convites.)		
Would you like to go to ...?		
...a barbecue	...a birthday party	...a restaurant
...the movies	...the club	...a party

1 Invite some friends to an event in your house. Give as much information as you can.
(Convide alguns amigos para um evento em sua casa. Dê o máximo de informações que puder.)

Create 2 possible answers to your invitation.

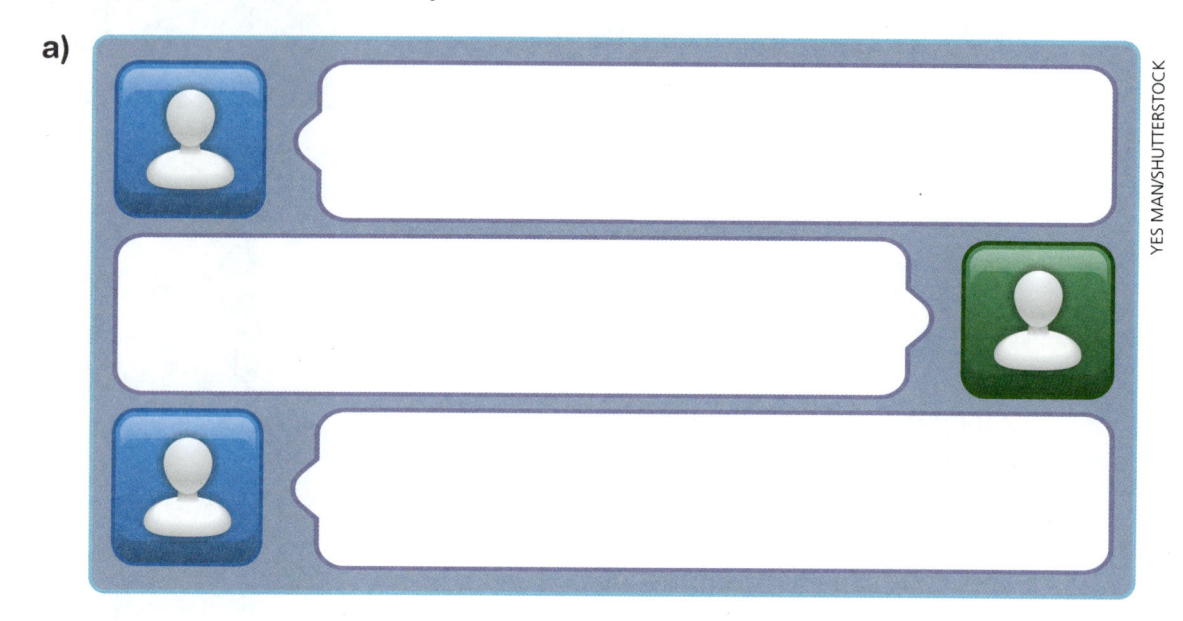

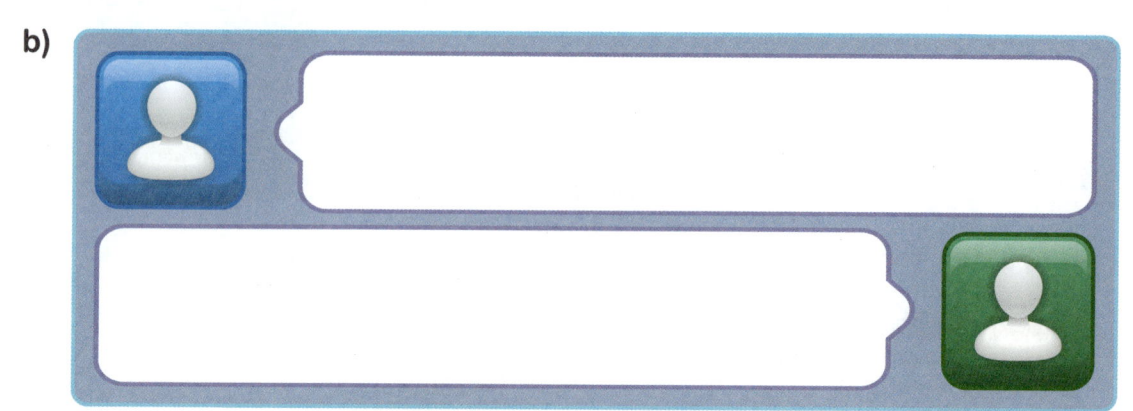

a)

b)

2 Answer the invitations.
(Responda aos convites.)

a) Would you like to go to my party?

Yes, _____.

b) Would you like to eat an ice cream?

No, _____.

> **I learned how to make plans for the future.**
> (Eu aprendi como fazer planos para o futuro.)
>
> – I **am going to** the supermarket tomorrow.

3 Write three things you plan to do on your vacation.
(Escreva três coisas que você planeja fazer nas suas férias.)

_____
_____
_____
_____

4 Write sentences with the adverbs of time and frequency you've learned.
(Escreva frases com os advérbios de tempo e frequência que você aprendeu.)

_____
_____
_____
_____
_____
_____
_____

GLOSSARY
(Glossário)

A

a lot of: muito(s), bastante
abolition: abolição
action: ação
afraid of: com medo
always: sempre
American: americano(a)
Argentinian: argentino(a)

B

back: de volta
barbecue: churrasco
basketball: basquete
beach: praia
bed: cama
believe: acreditar
birthday: aniversário
Brazilian: brasileiro(a)
brother: irmão
brush: escovar
build: construir

C

cartoon: desenho animado
celebrated: celebrou, celebrado(a)
Chinese: chinês, chinesa
choose: escolher
clean: limpar
climbing: escalar
cross: cruz
cycling: ciclismo

D

dad: papai
dangerous: perigoso(a)
discovery: descoberta
dishes: louça
diving: mergulhar
draw: desenhar
drink: bebida, beber

E

eat: comer
emotion: emoção
English: inglês, inglesa
every day: todo dia
excitement: excitação

F

farm: fazenda
fascinated: fascinado(a)
father: pai
favorite: favorito(a)
forget: esquecer
French: francês, francesa
friendly: amigável
friends: amigos(as)
from: de

G

garden: jardim
go: ir

H

hair: cabelo

hands: mãos
healthy: saudável
here: aqui
high: alto(a)
homework: lição de casa
horse riding: andar a cavalo
How often?: Com que frequência?

I

imagine: imaginar
interview: entrevista
invitation: convite
Italian: italiano(a)

J

Japanese: japonês, japonesa
juice: suco

K

kind: tipo
king: rei

L

land: terra
language: língua
letter: carta
Lisbon: Lisboa
listen: escutar, ouvir

M

make: fazer
mass: missa
Math: matemática
Mexican: mexicano(a)
milk: leite

mom: mamãe
month: mês
mother: mãe
mountain: montanha
movies: cinema, filmes
musical: musical

N

natives: nativos
never: nunca
next: próximo

P

paint: pintar
party: festa
peaceful: pacífico
people: pessoas, povo
place: lugar
play: jogar, tocar, brincar
Portuguese: português, portuguesa
prepared: preparado(a)

R

radical: radical
rafting: *rafting*
rappel: rapel
read: ler
relax: relaxar
ride: cavalgar
risk: risco
romance: romance
room: quarto
running: corrida
Russian: russo(a)

S

safe: seguro
sandwich: sanduíche
school: escola
science fiction: ficção científica
ships: navios
shower: chuveiro
singer: cantor(a)
sister: irmã
skiing: esquiar
small: pequeno(a)
soccer: futebol
soda: refrigerante
some: algum, alguns
sometimes: às vezes
space: espaço
speak: falar
sport: esporte
strangers: estranhos
strong: forte
study: estudar
summer camp: acampamento de verão
swim: nadar

T

tea: chá
teeth: dentes
tomorrow: amanhã
trainer: treinador

U

used to: costumava

V

vacation: férias
volleyball: vôlei

W

want: querer
wash: lavar
watch: assistir
water: água
week: semana
weekend: fim de semana
when: quando
where: onde
winds: ventos
windsurf: windsurfe
Would you like?: Você gostaria?
write: escrever

Y

yesterday: ontem

Amiguinhos, nas próximas páginas vocês encontrarão os complementos que serão utilizados em várias atividades deste livro.

Coleção

Eu gosto m@is

ALMANAQUE

MEMORY GAME

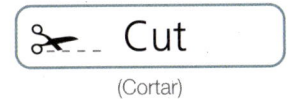

✂ Cut
(Cortar)

COMPLEMENTARY ACTIVITIES

Argentina	Argentina
Brazil	England	Italy
Brazil	England	Italy
Australia	China	France
Australia	China	France

99

Parte integrante da Coleção Eu Gosto M@is – Língua Inglesa 4º ano – IBEP.

Cut
(Cortar)

COMPLEMENTARY ACTIVITIES

Japan	Japan
Mexico	Nigeria	Portugal
Mexico	Nigeria	Portugal
Russia	Spain	United States of America
Russia	Spain	United States of America

Parte integrante da Coleção Eu Gosto M@is – Língua Inglesa 4º ano – IBEP.

101

CELEBRITIES

✂ Cut
(Cortar)

COMPLEMENTARY ACTIVITIES

Chris Pratt

Gal Gadot

Emma Watson

John Boyega

Parte integrante da Coleção Eu Gosto M@is – Língua Inglesa 4º ano – IBEP.

SURVEY

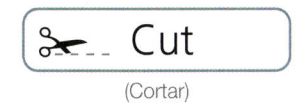

✂ Cut
(Cortar)

COMPLEMENTARY ACTIVITIES

Name: _____ Date: _____

a) What kind of drink do you like?

☐ soda ☐ juice ☐ water
☐ milk ☐ tea ☐ coffee

b) What kind of food do you like?

☐ pasta ☐ pizza ☐ salad
☐ hamburguer ☐ sandwich ☐ fruit

c) What kind of movies do you like?

☐ action ☐ cartoon ☐ science fiction
☐ romance ☐ comedy ☐ musical

d) What kind of sports do you like?

☐ soccer ☐ tennis ☐ volleyball
☐ cycling ☐ swimming ☐ basketball

e) What kind of dessert do you like?

☐ ice cream ☐ chocolate ☐ cake
☐ apple ☐ pudding ☐ pie

Parte integrante da Coleção Eu Gosto M@is – Língua Inglesa 4º ano – IBEP.

FREQUENCY ADVERBS

✂ Cut
(Cortar)

COMPLEMENTARY ACTIVITIES

He plays basketball every day.

She takes a bath every day.

She always goes to school.

He never sleeps late.

ILUSTRAÇÕES: LYUDMYLA KHARLAMOVA/SHUTTERSTOCK

107

Parte integrante da Coleção Eu Gosto M@is – Língua Inglesa 4º ano – IBEP.

USED TO AND DIDN'T USE TO

✂ Cut
(Cortar)

COMPLEMENTARY ACTIVITIES

ILUSTRAÇÕES: LYUDMYLA KHARLAMOVA/SHUTTERSTOCK

play with teddy bear

ride a tricycle

play with toy cars

play with dolls

play with toy instruments

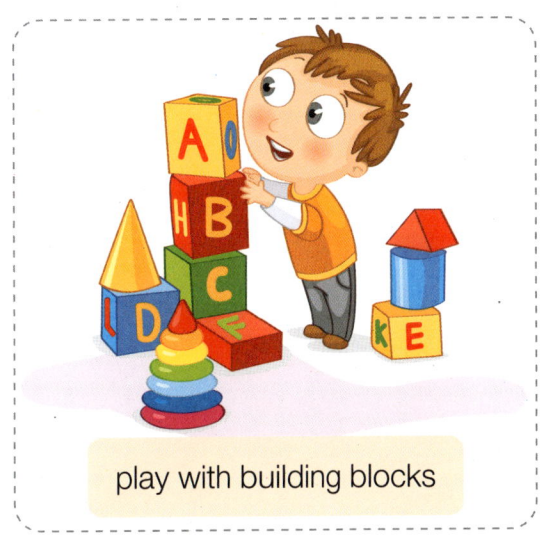

play with building blocks

Parte integrante da Coleção Eu Gosto M@is – Língua Inglesa 4º ano – IBEP.

GOING TO

✂ Cut
(Cortar)

COMPLEMENTARY ACTIVITIES

watch a movie

play on the beach

go to summer camp

go to a farm

play video games

visit my grandmother

111

Parte integrante da Coleção Eu Gosto M@is – Língua Inglesa 4º ano – IBEP.